DATE DUE

SCHOLASTIC
News
Nonfiction Readers

Pluto
Dwarf Planet

by
Christine Taylor-Butler

Children's Press
An Imprint of Scholastic Inc.
New York Toronto London Auckland Sydney
Mexico City New Delhi Hong Kong
Danbury, Connecticut

These content vocabulary word builders
are for grades 1–2.

Consultant: Michelle Yehling, Astronomy Education Consultant

The image on the cover is an artist's rendition of Pluto.

Photo Credits:

Photographs © 2008: DK Images: 4 top, 13; NASA: 11 (John Hopkins University Applied Physics Laboratory/ Southwest Research Institute), 23 bottom (A. Schaller/ ESA), cover, 5 top right and bottom right, 10; Photo Researchers, NY: 2, 5 top left (Chris Butler), 1, 4 bottom right, 7 (Lynette Cook), back cover, 19 (Lynette Cook/SPL), 23 top (Mark Garlick), 15 (NASA/ESA/STScI), 5 bottom left, 9 (Deltev van Ravenswaay).

Illustration Credits:

Illustration pages 20–21 by Greg Harris

Illustrations page 4, 17 by Pat Rasch

Book Design: Simonsays Design!
Book Production: The Design Lab

Library of Congress Cataloging-in-Publication Data
Taylor-Butler, Christine.
Pluto : dwarf planet / By Christine Taylor-Butler.—Updated ed.
   p. cm.—(Scholastic news nonfiction readers)
Includes bibliographical references and index.
ISBN-13: 978-0-531-14751-1 (lib.bdg.)   978-0-531-14766-5 (pbk.)
ISBN-10: 0-531-14751-7 (lib. bdg.)   0-531-14766-5 (pbk.)
1. Pluto (Dwarf planet)—Juvenile literature. I. Title.
QB701.T39 2008
523.48'2—dc22   2006102779

CONTENTS

WORD HUNT

Look for these words as you read. They will be in **bold**.

core
(kor)

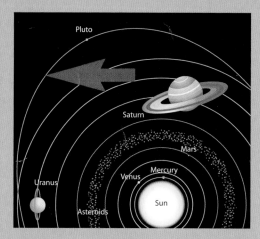

orbit
(**or**-bit)

Pluto
(**ploo**-toh)

4

moon
(moon)

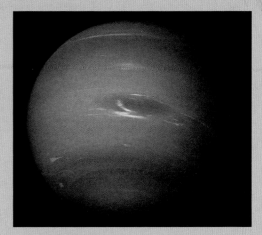

Neptune
(**nep**-toon)

solar system
(**oh**-lur **siss**-tuhm)

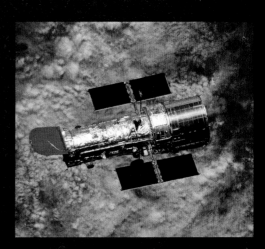

telescope
(**tel**-uh-skope)

Pluto!

Pluto is very far away.

Some pictures have been taken of Pluto. But in them, the surface of Pluto is hard to see.

Many pictures of Pluto are painted by artists.

An artist drew this picture of Pluto.

Pluto is a dwarf planet.

Dwarf planets are round like planets. But they are smaller. The space around them is full of smaller objects.

The area around planets is mostly empty.

Both planets and dwarf planets are found in the **solar system**.

Pluto

Sun

9

Pluto is farther from the Sun than all the planets.

It is hard to see even with a giant space **telescope**.

In 2006, a spaceship called *New Horizons* left for Pluto. It won't arrive until 2015!

telescope

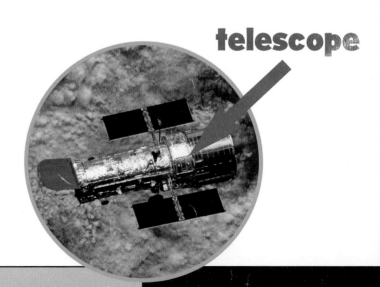

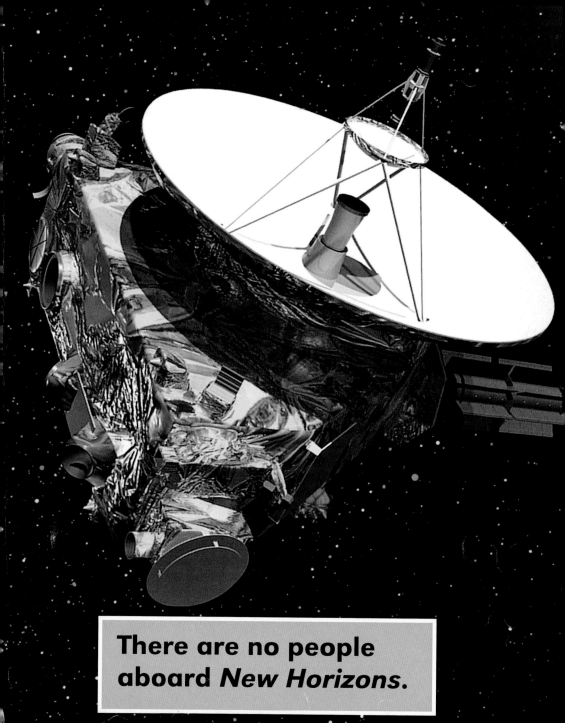

There are no people aboard *New Horizons*.

Scientists know that
Pluto is made of both
rock and ice.

The outside of Pluto is
mostly solid ice.

The inside is called
the **core**.

Scientists are not sure
how much of the core is
rock or ice.

core

Earth has one **moon**. Pluto has three.

They are called Charon, Hydra, and Nix.

Charon and Pluto look alike. They both look like icy balls, but Charon is smaller than Pluto.

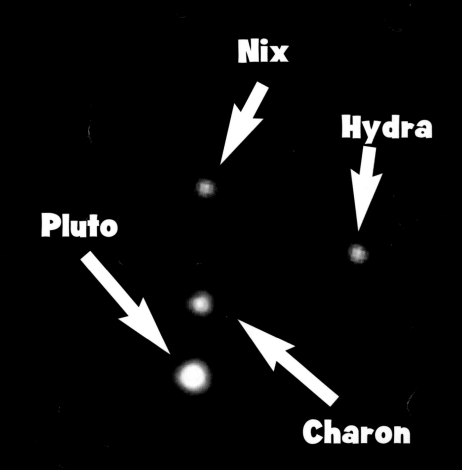

Nix

Hydra

Pluto

Charon

Charon is about half the size of Pluto.

Pluto goes around the Sun on a path called an **orbit**.

Pluto's path is shaped more like an oval than most planets' orbits.

Sometimes Pluto's orbit crosses **Neptune's** orbit. But Pluto and Neptune will never hit each other.

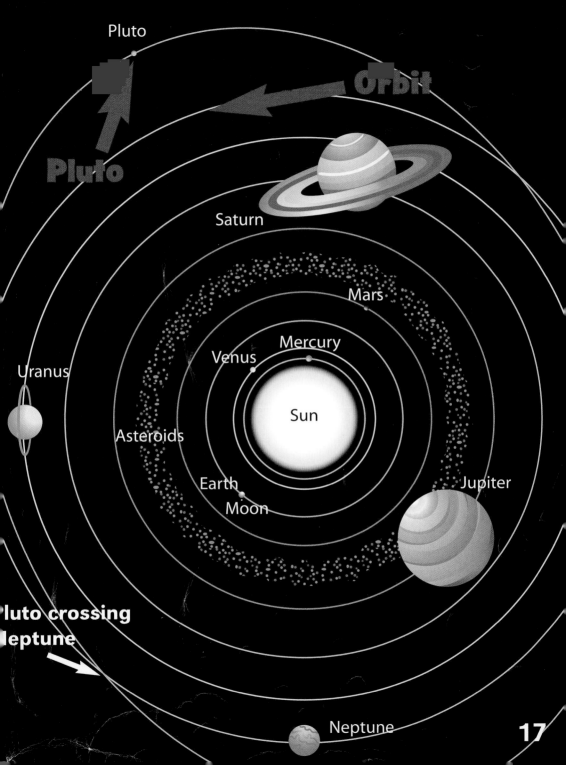

Pluto

Orbit

Pluto

Saturn

Mars

Mercury

Venus

Uranus

Sun

Asteroids

Earth
Moon

Jupiter

Pluto crossing
Neptune

Neptune

In 2226, Pluto will cross Neptune's orbit.

But Pluto will still be far away.

From the surface of Pluto, the Sun will still look as small as a star.

Will we know what Pluto really looks like by 2226?

Maybe!

Sun

Pluto

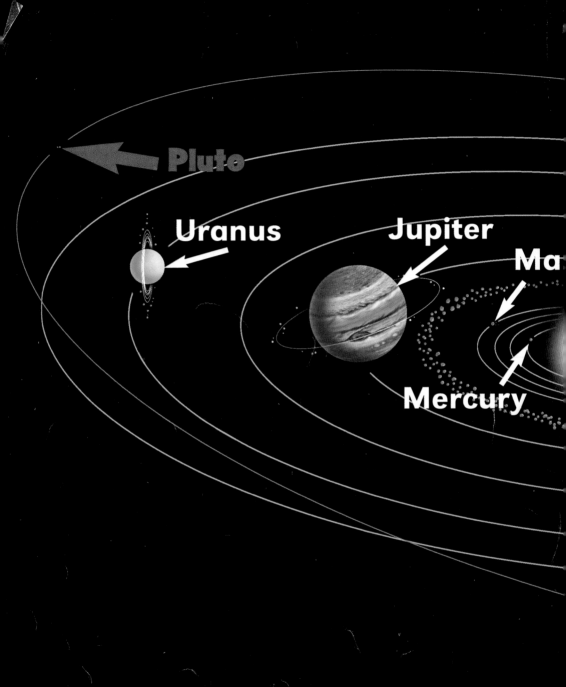

Pluto

Uranus

Jupiter

Ma

Mercury

PLUTO
IN OUR SOLAR SYSTEM

Sun

Venus

Saturn

Earth

Neptune

YOUR NEW WORDS

core (kor) the inside of an object

moon (moon) an object that
circles a larger object

Neptune (**nep**-toon) a planet named after
the Roman god of the sea

orbit (**or**-bit) the path an object takes
around another object

Pluto (**ploo**-toh) a dwarf planet
named after the Roman god of
the underworld

solar system (**soh**-lur **siss**-tuhm) the
group of planets, dwarf planets,
moons, and other things that travel
around the Sun

telescope (**tel**-uh-skope) a tool used to
see things far away

Other Dwarf Planets

Ceres is found in an area between Mars and Jupiter called the Asteroid Belt.

Eris is in the Kuiper Belt, a ring of icy rocks outside the orbit of Neptune.

INDEX

FIND OUT MORE

Book:
Burnham, Robert. *Children's Atlas of the Universe.* Pleasantville, NY: Reader's Digest Children's Publishing, Inc., 2000.

Web site:
Solar System Exploration
http://sse.jpl.nasa.gov/planets

MEET THE AUTHOR

Christine Taylor-Butler is the author of more than twenty books for children. She holds a degree in Engineering from M.I.T. She lives in Kansas City with her family, where they have a telescope for searching the skies.